HEADS AND TALES

*A Collection of the True
and the Trivial*

Alastair Gordon,
Marquess of Aberdeen

*Illustrations by
Anne Gordon,
Marchioness of Aberdeen*

The Book Guild Ltd
Sussex, England

The Book Guild Ltd
25 High Street,
Lewes, Sussex

First published 1999
Second printing 1999
Third printing 2000

Set in Baskerville

Typesetting by Keyboard Services, Luton, Beds

Printed in Great Britain by
Bookcraft (Bath) Ltd, Avon

A catalogue record for this book is
available from the British Library

ISBN 1 85776 486 2

CONTENTS

INTRODUCTION

In 1929, my grandfather, then aged 82, published a short book with the title *Jokes Cracked by Lord Aberdeen*. They are jocular Victorian jokes, a bit heavy-handed, but some of them genuinely funny. He would tell these jokes in a pedantic high-pitched voice.

My family have persuaded me to set down some of *my* jokes.

There is a problem here. The written word and the spoken word need quite different styles.

Obviously what I have written comes out differently when one becomes a raconteur. Accent, inflexion and timing must be directed toward the punchline. Gestures (or sometimes lack of them) must be apt and descriptive, body language (and again, possibly, lack of it) must point towards the denouement. Surprise is the key. Above all, when telling a joke, don't laugh at it yourself.

Significantly, the finest raconteurs are professional character actors. They are natural show-offs, they have learnt dialect with a sharp ear, and they *rehearse*. In particular, their timing is polished and immaculate. A good tale, badly told, becomes a lead balloon, and becomes even more leaden if told to the wrong type of audience. Some dirty jokes can be appealing to one group of people, but offensive to another – you must choose carefully. Telling them with sly lasciviousness is plain awful and embarrassing however tolerant your audience is of sexual or lavatorial jokes. Worse still is the under-rehearsed telling: you must learn a laid-back but fluent delivery.

Some of these stories are my own originals. *All* the anecdotes are either personal experiences or given to me first-hand. But most of the stories have been told me by others or are culled from scholarly 'commonplace' books by men who liked storing wit and wisdom.

Whichever category they are, there will inevitably be people who say 'Oh God, I heard that one years ago'. But *most* of them will be new for *most* people, and that is my justification for putting them on record.

An Awful Warning

These quotes were always in the forefront of my mind during my 40 years of writing art criticism.

There was, perhaps, in Constable, the making of a second or third rate painter, if any careful discipline had developed in him the instincts, which, though unparalleled for narrowness, were in fact, as far as they went, true. But, as it is, he is nothing more than an industrious and innocent amateur, blundering his way to a superficial expression of one or two aspects of common nature.

John Ruskin in 1856

The death penalty is a great evil, since but for it I should probably have murdered a large number of people, and we would now be plagued by fewer of those pernicious fools who are the bane of art and artists.

Berlioz

SEX / THE BODY

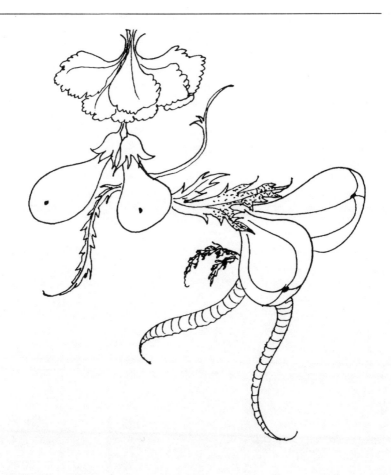

A class in a boarding school were told to write a story about being frugal. One child asked what frugal meant and the teacher said 'It means to be careful, about saving – in other words, to save.' The child thought for a bit and then wrote:

> In the olden time a knight was riding his trusty white horse and he came by a wood. He heard the cries of a damsel in distress. He spurred his horse into the wood, and there, in a clearing, was a beautiful girl tied to a tree, being threatened by a fiery dragon.
>
> 'Frugal me, frugal me!' she cried. And he frugalled her and they lived happily ever after.

Two young Irishmen were walking in their village. Passing the church, one of them said, 'I want to go to confession and get absolution from Father O'Leary.'

While the friend waited outside the other went to the confessional:

'Well, my son,' said the good father, 'and what have you come to confess?'

'Fornication, father,' said the young man.

'Oh, indeed, and was it with Jane O'Reilly?'

'No, father.'

'Then was it Rose McCormick?'

'No, no, father, I cannot tell you who it was.'

'Well,' said Father O'Leary, becoming cross, 'I cannot give you absolution if you do not co-operate. Be off with you!'

When the young man came out his friend asked, 'Did you get absolution?'

'No,' said his friend, 'but I got two very good leads.'

A. P. Herbert, author, poet, wit and maverick MP, is thought to be the writer of these verses:

The portions of a woman that appeal to man's
   depravity
Are fashioned with considerable care,
And what at first appears to be a simple little cavity
Is really an elaborate affair.

Now, doctors who have bothered to study these
   phenomena
In numbers of experimental dames
Have made a list of all things in the feminine
   abdomina
And given them delightful Latin names.

There's the vulva, the vagina and the jolly perineum
And the hymen which is found in certain brides,
And many other things you'd like if only you could
   see 'em
The clitoris, and Lord-knows-what besides!

Now isn't it a pity when we common people chatter
Of the mysteries to which I have referred,
That we use in such a delicate and complicated matter
Such a short and unattractive little word.

4

I had a letter published in the *Daily Telegraph* about upmarket brothels in London and Paris during the 1940s and 1950s.
A friend sent me this:

> The Marquess of Aberdeen
> Was occasionally to be seen
> Playing the cello
> In a Paris bordello.

Practice *Safe Sex!*

A little boy asked his father: 'Papa, when you and mama went on your honeymoon in Italy, where was I?'

To which his father replied; 'You went there with me, and came back with your mother.'

Picture a blustery summer's day in the Bois de Boulogne in Paris.

Amongst those walking about is a splendid old gentleman: immaculate suit, curly-brimmed grey bowler hat, lavender gloves, silver-topped walking stick. Coming towards him on the path is a beautiful young girl in a red dress with a flared skirt.

A sudden gust of wind whips up her red skirt to reveal enchanting black underclothes. The old boy's eyes nearly pop out.

'*Ah, m'sieur,*' says the girl archly, '*rouge et noir!*'

The bowler hat is raised courteously, then a sad shake of the head.

'*Oui, m'selle, mais – hélas – rien ne va plus.*'

(When telling this, make sure your listeners know the argot of roulette.)

Two cowboys had been out on the range for weeks. They came to a township which one of them knew very well. 'When we hit town,' he said to his companion, 'we'll go to the liquor store where there is a gorgeous dame serving behind the counter. I will ask her for the raisin wine, which is on the top shelf and she has to go climb a ladder, and – oh, boy – you can see right up her skirts.'

And so it came about just as he said. The girl turned to the other cowboy and said, 'Is yours a raisin too?'

'No, ma' am, just a-twirlin' and a-twitchin'.'

Have you not in a chimney seen
A sullen faggot wet and green
How coyly it receives the heat
And at both ends doth fume and sweat.

So fares it with the gentle maid
When first upon her back she's laid
But the kind experienced dame
Cracks and rejoices in the flame.

The Earl of Rochester

I wonder if Lord Rochester was conversant with the ancient Chinese sexology manuscripts where 'rejoices' is the euphemism for female orgasm.

A Crusader knight locked up his wife's chastity belt, gave the key for safe keeping to his best friend, and trotted off down the Dover road to catch the ferry to the Holy Land.

Halfway through Kent he heard the pounding of galloping hooves coming up fast behind him. The rider reined in with a cloud of dust.

It was the best friend. 'Wrong key,' he said, holding it up.

A true story.

A recently qualified lady doctor got a job with a medical practice near Liverpool.

She resolved to be brisk and businesslike in order to impress her working-class patients, so when the first came in – a man – she said firmly: 'Now, what is the matter with you?'

'Well, it's me seat, doctor.'

'Very well, take down your trousers and get on the couch facing the wall.'

She then carried out a detailed rectal examination and said: 'You can get dressed, there's nothing the matter with you.'

The man pulled up his trousers, and then, pointing at his eyes, said: 'Hey, doc, you've got me wrong. It's me *seet* – I can't see.'

Another medical story, this one bizarre.

A gynaecologist whose problem was that he was very shy, habitually examined women through a curtain to hide his embarrassment. To one lady he mumbled diffidently, 'Would you open your legs wider, please?'

Nothing happened so he repeated the behest. Still no movement, so, desperation overcoming his shyness he said loudly, 'Would you open your legs wider!'

The woman said, 'Oh, I'm so sorry, I thought you were talking to the nurse.'

Cyril Connolly's aphorism that in every fat man there is a thin one trying to get out is better known than the follow-up: 'Outside every thin woman is a fat man trying to get in.'

The Bishop of Exeter, addressing a girls' school after attending there a performance of *A Midsummer Night's Dream*, said: 'It's the first time I have ever seen a female Bottom.'

A house party of 16 decided to play nebbers (charades without speech) after a vinous dinner party. The eight ladies went out to prepare their act. They came back into the drawing room naked, and lined up thus: the first facing the men, the second back, the third facing, then another back, the fifth facing, and the remaining three back.

The men, admiring this display but quite defeated, finally gave up. The answer was the overture to *William Tell* – titty bum, titty bum, titty bum bum bum.

NOTABLE PEOPLE

When my wife and I became engaged, by happenchance the first person to propose our health was Augustus John. The brilliant, but drunkenly bleary, blue eyes looked her up and down approvingly, and then, in a slurred voice he pronounced, 'Now we must think of an app-rop-ri-ate lit-er-ary toast,' and slumped back in his chair, asleep. So we never got the toast.

When John was painting his famous picture of Madame Suggia playing the 'cello, he noticed at the beginning of one sitting that her eyes were fixed disdainfully at a point on the floor. He looked – and saw there a used condom. He put down his palette and brushes, picked up the fire tongs, opened the door of the stove, and disposed of the offensive object. No word was said, and the sitting continued as if nothing had happened.

Two true stories of the great Lord Derby, Knight of the Garter, Privy Councillor, and Minister for War in 1916. He loved his food and in old age more and more so.

One day, leaving Knowsley after a rich lunch, he had difficulty climbing into his Rolls-Royce.

This was the opportunity his chauffeur had been waiting for: he had been teased by his fellow Rolls-Royce chauffeurs who said, 'How come you have such an old-fashioned

Rolls when your employer is one of the richest men in the land?'

'The new model has wider doors, m'lord,' said the chauffeur.

'Get it,' said Derby, waving a hand, 'get it.'

Recorded by Randolph Churchill in his life of Derby was the time when the very civilised Lord Kenyon had stayed at Knowsley. He made admiring remarks about the Old Master paintings, the superb furniture and anything else that was magnificent.

'Make sure Kenyon never comes to stay again,' said Derby to his agent. 'He *noticed my things*.'

Randolph's comment on this was – 'it's not true to say that Lord Derby had bad taste, he had no taste at all.'

A retired ambassador with a brilliant and accurate mind told me a story that had come down to him through court circles.

The royal yacht, the *Victoria and Albert*, was at anchor – sometime in the early 1900s. A group of equerries and ADCs quite accidentally overheard from the King's stateroom: 'Get another pillow under your bum, and stop calling me Sir!'

The definition of a Hungarian (said a Hungarian) is a person who goes into a revolving door behind you and comes out in front.

The Empress Elizabeth of Austria enjoyed staying in England for the hunting, bringing a large entourage of Austro-Hungarian nobility with her.

On one of these visits she was staying with the Duke of Portland. An Englishman in the house party said, by way of conversation, to Count Csaky, 'Do you know, the Duke has a million sheep on his estates, how many have you got?'

'I do not know how many sheep I have,' Count Csaky replied thoughtfully, 'but I do know I have a million sheepdogs.'

Osbert Lancaster was a close friend whose conversation was splendidly orotund. It was difficult to memorise, so thick and fast came the phrases, but one story stands out particularly. He told me how the first of Graham Sutherland's portraits (of Beaverbrook) came about.

'The people at the *Express* came to me, as the only person on the paper who could read and write, and told me they wanted a portrait done of the Beaver. I said ask Graham Sutherland; apart from the certainty that it would be a good painting I thought of it as an interesting confrontation between an enthusiastic Roman Catholic convert and a lapsed Calvinist with a keen interest in theology.'

On another occasion we were discussing Verdi's *Otello* and praising it fulsomely. Osbert summed up with: 'We are agreed that we prefer the musical to the play'.

'Good King Wenceslas' was transcribed by Osbert Lancaster in suitable modern English, in the form of a despatch from HBM Ambassador in Prague to the Foreign Office.

DISTRIBUTION

H. of C. ✓

H. ✓

Central Dept. F.O.
for attention
Ministry of Fuel
and Power ✓

Foreign Relations
Div./Min. /
F. & P. /

Research Dept.
Min. of F. & P.

Lord Cherwell,
for O.U.S.

C.O.I. (Religious
Div.)

National Gas
Board

British Council

M.I.5

Archbishop of
Canterbury, to
see.

Whose fuel allocation it is not clear.

Have the Forestry Comm'n seen this?? No! Why not?

On the 26th inst the Chief Executive was making an
ploratory reconnaissance in the field under wintry condi
tions with good visibility but considerable iceing-up wh
unit of lower income bracket personnel entered his field
vision unauthorisedly supplementing his seasonal fuel al
cation. A request for information from his P.A. as to th
identity of the agricultural worker elicited the informa
that he, the agricultural worker, was normally resident
three statutory miles (approx) from the point of referen
at the foot of rising ground in close proximity to the
clearly defined boundary of the nationalized timber plan
tion in the immediate neighbourhood of a water supply di
tribution point scheduled as a National Monument under th
Act (q.v. "St. Agnes" Fountain). The C.E. putting in a
formal request for a supplementary allowance of meat, im
ported alcoholic beverages and soft-wood said, that they
the C.E. and his P.A., would personally supervise his, th
agricultural worker's, food-intake after having effected
transfer of the aforesaid supplementary rations. The C.E
and his P.A. thereupon proceeded in company through a win

16

of exceptional velocity and subnormal temperature conditions.

The P.A. drew the attention of the C.E. to the worsening of nocturnal visibility and the increased wind-velocity. He said that owing to a constitutional cardiac condition of unknown origin he was not in a position to proceed further. The C.E. instructed his P.A. to pin-point the soil disturbance caused by his, the C.E.'s feet and to unhesitatingly adapt them to his own means of progress: in which case the Personal Assistant would become aware that his circulatory deficiency rendered him less susceptible to climatic disturbance.

The Personal Assistant in accordance with instruction placed his feet in conformity with the impressions retained by the snow: the actual subsoil proved to be thermostatically controlled by direct recent contact with the canonised C.E.

In view of the above the attention of all males (C. of E.) in the higher income groups and/or of established executive grade at departmental level is drawn to the fact that a reasonable degree of certainty would seem to attach to the proposition that reciprocal advantages are likely to accrue to those taking a practical interest in the amelioration of social conditions pertaining to lower grade manual employment.

Industrial Relations Attache's Office
H. M. EMBASSY, PRAGUE.

Lancaster

[Handwritten marginal annotations:]

Do the Air Ministry confirm this? C

Still awaiting reply to our communication of 3rd ult. Jm.

Ministry of labour usage? H.E.

The use of semi-military slang which is noticeable in minutes from the Service attaches is MOST out of place in communications from the Ind. Rels. Office. J.L.

A clear case of adjectival remote control. Q

Must the young gentlemen in the F.O. display their graphic abilities on every file that reaches this Dept??! C

Propaganda ?? Jm.

I feel strongly that no release should be given to the Press without prior consultation with the Archbishop and M.I.5. H.E.

Too late !! see this morning's Times

I agree HT.

How about the B.B.C.? AW.

No blotting paper in our Prague Embassy?

[printed at bottom right:] Pen and Ink reproduction

17

This was given me by the same ambassador who told me the *V&A* story.

H.M. EMBASSY
MOSCOW

Lord Pembroke
The Foreign Office
LONDON   6th April 1943

My Dear Reggie,

In these dark days man tends to look for little shafts of light that spill from Heaven. My days are probably darker than yours, and I need. my God I do, all the light I can get. But I am a decent fellow, and I do not want to be mean and selfish about what little brightness is shed upon me from time to time. So I propose to share with you a tiny flash that has illuminated my sombre life and tell you that God has given me a new Turkish colleague whose card tells me that he, is called Mustapha Kunt.

We all feel like that, Reggie, now and then, especially when Spring is upon us, but few of us would care to put it on our cards. It takes a Turk to do that.

Sir Archibald Clerk Kerr,
·H.M. Ambassador.

When Whistler first exhibited his painting *Symphony in White* a critic complained that although the girl was wearing a white dress there were other colours surrounding her.

'And does he, in his astounding consequence,' screamed the painter, 'think that a symphony in F is the repetition of the note FFF!'

This charming piece of gossip was handed on by a grand elderly lady at the beginning of the Queen's reign.

She was a guest at Balmoral during the annual royal visit. The Moderator of the General Assembly of the Church of Scotland had been invited to dine. A delightful old-fashioned gentleman, he appeared even more archaic in his buttoned frock coat, knee-breeches, black stockings and silver buckled shoes.

When he came to leave, the Queen enquired whether he had enjoyed himself. 'Oh, yes, Ma'am,' he replied. 'I had happy intercourse with Lady Salisbury on the sofa.'

The suppressed giggles became uncontrollable laughter after the door had closed.

'The trouble with you lot,' said the Duke of Edinburgh, 'is you all have dirty minds.'

I met Terry Thomas in a bar in Le Lavandou in 1947, when that resort was an unpretentious village. He was delighted to make friends with people who had never heard of him. Every night we foregathered in this bar, and to a small audience of half a dozen or so (including his wife) we realised quickly what a master raconteur he was.

Here is one that I remember (to be told with a Welsh intonation).

Mrs Evans went to Mr Jones's butcher's shop.

'Good morning, Mr Jones,' she said, 'and what a cold morning it is!'

'Indeed, Mrs Evans, do you know when I opened up the shop this morning the testicles were hanging down eighteen inches long.'

That afternoon Mrs Morgan came in.

'What a cold day it is, is it not, Mr Jones?'

'Yes indeed, when I opened up the shop this morning the icicles were hanging down eighteen inches long.'

'That is not what you said to my sister Mrs Evans this morning.'

'I know, I made a proper bollocks of that, didn't I?'

The story, as told by Terry Thomas, would fill three pages of this book. The amateur raconteur should attempt nothing longer than the bare bones that I have set down.

This is a true Churchill story.

A friend of mine was G2 War Cabinet Staff when Churchill went in the *Queen Mary* to visit Roosevelt, who came out in the cruiser USS *Augusta*.

My friend had a large map, in a room on the ship, of all the land battle fronts: his job was to mark up the sitrep (situation report) of what was happening to the armies engaged.

On the opposite side of the room was a naval officer with an equally large map of the oceans on which he charted known naval movements.

Late every night Winston would come in with Beaverbrook, each holding a balloon glass of brandy.

On one of these nights the naval officer indicated the direction of a wolf pack of U-boats and that it and the *Queen Mary* would coincide at about 2am.

'Beaver,' said Winston, 'we must stay awake. What do you recommend? More brandy? Or less brandy?'

This same friend was alone in the War Cabinet room with Winston late at night. He had given a sitrep to the Prime Minister, who thought for a bit, and said:

'That idle First Army and its incompetent commander. I have a mind to take a plane and go and beat him up.'

And then – 'Take paper.' (And my friend took a sheet of paper headed 10 Downing Street. He poised, pen in hand.)

'Message from Prime Minister to General Alexander – General Ike is becoming pusillanimous, pray motivate him.'

As an example of Winston's utter disregard for convention by confiding this kind of opinion to a mere major, it is hard to beat.

It was a tradition that King Gustavus of Sweden shot a moose on Christmas Day. However, as the king became older and increasingly infirm, the moose shoot had to become stage-managed until eventually the old king would be seated on the balcony of the palace whilst a reliably placid moose would be led within range and duly shot. One year the moose understandably made a run for it, leaving the game-keeper frantically waving his arms, shouting, 'I'm NOT the moose' – at which point King Gustavus lifted his gun and fired, narrowly missing the chap. A perplexed courtier asked the king why he had shot at the gamekeeper when he had been shouting 'I am NOT the moose.' 'Good Lord,' replied King Olaf, 'I thought he was shouting I AM the moose.'

Leon Goossens, the great oboist, told me that Malcolm Sargent (a renowned snob) invited him to the green room after a concert. There was a languid figure lying on the sofa.

'I must introduce my great friend the King of Sweden,' said Sargent.

'Norway,' said a tired voice from the sofa.

This was told me by the director of Heinemann's, who was editing Randolph Churchill's first volumes of the life of Winston.

In 1944 Randolph, with Evelyn Waugh and others, was camped in a mountain cave in Yugoslavia, where they were directing the supply of arms to Tito.

One day two studious young American officers arrived bearing gifts for Tito – a jeep (useful), and a film of the American way of life.

They turned to Randolph and asked, 'What kind of a man is this Marshal Tito?'

'Oh! She's rather a jolly old lady,' interposed Evelyn Waugh.

The Americans replied, 'We have it on the best authority that when Marshal Tito visited your General Alexander at Caserta Palace he slept every night with his beautiful lady secretary.'

'But,' said Waugh – warming to the task of teasing these earnest Americans – 'I thought *everybody* knew she was a lesbian.'

I was told this story by Maurice Macmillan, who presumably got it first-hand from his father Harold.

When Churchill became PM again in 1951 he had new men in the Cabinet as well as a few old hands. So, they were all agog and waiting for the great man's opening remarks, which were:

'Gentlemen, I have two very serious matters to tell you about – first, Lord Jowett has been made an earl' – pause, and a hand raised – 'but worse is to follow … Herbert Morrison has been made a Companion of *Honour*. We will now turn to more frivolous subjects such as the situation in the Middle East.'

RHYMES

The tits of a typist at Auteuil
Were caressed by some hands in a fauteuil.
But she cried 'I've been wronged!'
When she found they belonged
To a lesbian wearing a bauteuil.

There was a young lady of Ryde
Who ate apples and apples and died
The apples fermented
Inside the lamented
And made cider inside 'er inside.

Said the Duchess of Alba to Goya
Pray recall that I am your employer
So he once made her pose
In magnificent clothes
And once in the nude to annoy her.

When Alcibiades
Met Naiades
He would remove the bodices
Of those delightful goddesses

A man was bet he could not make up a limerick about a helicopter. He came up with this:

> A man met a girl and he stopped her
> And said that he'd like to adopt her
> The girl turned to fly
> But the man was too spry,
> He pursued her, and by Hell he cop't her.

If you ever get trapped amongst a bunch of half-drunk bores telling dirty limericks, each trying to cap the one before, tell them this one – it never fails to break the sequence:

> There was a young man of Dundee
> Who was stung on the hand by a wasp.
> When asked if it hurt
> He said not in the least
> But thank God it wasn't a hornet.

When I was working in a London office I was sent a printed card by a friend which read, in Old English script:

The Ten Properties of a Woman

The 1 is to be mery of chere
The 2 is to be well paced
The 3 to have a brode forheade
The 4 to have brode buttocks
The 5 to be harde of worde
The 6 to be easy to leap upon
The 7 to be good at longe jorney
The 8 to be well sturringe under a man
The 9 to be always busy with the mouth
The 10 ever to be chouppinge on the brydd

I showed the card to the prettiest of our secretaries, and scarcely half an hour later she came to my room and handed me a neatly typewritten reply:

Ten Most Vital 'Musts' of Men

They must:

1 be handsome of face
2 be rich of wallet
3 be slender of build
4 be unloving towards wife
5 be connoisseur of women
6 be gentle of touch
7 be unsharp of teeth
8 be soft of tongue
9 be easy to deceive
10 be enamoured of ME

I did not rise to this encouraging bait.

Dear Children

I'm sending you this to remind you
That taxes have taken away
The things that I found essential
My reindeer, my workshop, my sleigh.

I now make my rounds on a donkey
Who's old and crippled and slow
So you'll know if you don't see me this Christmas
That I'm out on my ass in the snow.

Yours sincerely,
Father Christmas

CRICKET

Told me by a *very* eminent cricket executive.

Northants v. Yorkshire when Tyson (the fastest bowler ever) and Fred Trueman (not much slower) were on opposing sides, became a test of nerve for the batsmen.

Wardle, the Yorkshire spin bowler, was bowled neck and crop by a Tyson cannonball.

As Trueman – the next man in – passed Wardle he said, 'That was a bloody awful shot.'

Next ball, Trueman's stumps were also uprooted. When he got back to the pavilion Wardle greeted him with 'An' that was a bloody awful shot an all, too', to which Trueman said, ''Appen to slip on pile of shit left in t'crease.'

Trueman *always* had to have the last word.

Another cricket story – this is such an old chestnut that many younger readers may not have heard it.

The Kent wicketkeeper of the Edwardian period was Huish. When he retired he went to watch a village game in Sussex. The local team were short of a wicketkeeper, so Huish volunteered and took the field. The captain told this unknown volunteer that he had better stand back as the opening bowler was pretty quick.

Huish declined this advice and stood up. The first ball fizzed past the batsman on the off side:

Huish took it with his right hand and threw it back. The

second ball fizzed by on the leg side: Huish took it with his left hand and threw it back.

Next ball the batsman lunged forward, missed, and quick as a flash Huish had the bails off.

'HOW WAS THAT!' he demanded.

'Bloody marvellous,' said the square leg umpire.

In the 1920s and 1930s, when Yorkshire cricket was in its golden age, there were no greater supporters than the Wilson family. On one dreadful third day it was plain that Yorkshire were going down to defeat by Essex. The Wilson family, unable to bear it, left the pavilion and went home before the end. Some friends of mine nearby noticed that one of the Wilsons had left behind a briefcase. So they took it home and began to ring them up to say they had it safely. (In those days telephones were manual and all calls went through a local exchange.)

The girl on the Wilsons' exchange said, 'Eh, doan't be daft, yer can't get through to t'Wilsons. Yorkshire's been beat, they've pulled ploog out.'

Another cricket story – a tall tale?

A batsman became famous for sometimes batting right-handed, sometimes left-handed, seemingly on a whim.

Eventually his best friend asked what decided him.

'Quite simple,' he said. 'When I wake up to go to a match I look at my wife, and if she is lying on her right side I bat right-handed, and left-handed if she is on her left side.'

'Then,' asked the friend, 'what do you do if she is lying on her back?'

'I ring up the ground and tell them I'll be twenty minutes late.'

34

A cricket match between two *very* rural sides reached a critical point when the vicar of one village was batting, and the vicar of the other was umpiring.

The bowler bowled, the batsman made a swipe, there was a click, the wicketkeeper caught it, and appealed loudly.

'Out,' said the umpire.

'No, no,' said the batsman, 'it didn't touch my bat, it was my pad that it touched.'

'Still out,' said the umpire, 'l.b.w.'

There was a distinct froideur between the two men of God for years.

MUSIC

In the first half of 1946 I was stationed at the 8th Corps HQ in Schleswig Holstein. The Headquarters were in the old summer palace of the kings of Denmark in the small town of Plön.

Here I met Theo Peters, a fluent German speaker in the Intelligence Corps who had made friends with the music establishment – British and German – in Hamburg. When we discovered that we had a mutual love for music, he took me to meet them. I met Theo Herrmann, the principal bass of the Hamburg State Opera, and also the formidably brainy Major Howard Hartog, who was in charge of the British Forces Network, where Captain Trevor Harvey (later to take on the successful Robert Meyer children's concerts at the Festival Hall) conducted the orchestra, Private James Gibb played the piano, and Aircraftsman Geraint Evans sang. I got pleasantly caught up with all this dazzling talent every week-end in Hamburg.

It was British and Germans combining to make music, and it was heady stuff for me to meet great stars of German opera as well as our own native emerging stars.

Then the greatest star of all, Elizabeth Schumann, came – her first visit for years – to give a recital at the Musikhalle. It was a regal event and had to be celebrated.

Howard Hartog, Trevor Harvey and Theo Peters organised a party for her and roped me in as a co-host because, as a Guards officer, I had access to unlimited quantities of wine. (When the Guards Armoured Division liberated Brussels we captured six million bottles of French wine labelled 'Reserve für Wehrmacht'.)

The party was held in the large, L-shaped drawing-room of a house in the centre of the city that had survived the fire-bomb destruction.

The great lady sat on a sofa flanked by Theo Herrmann and the conductor Hans Schmidt-Isserstedt. When I came to talk to her I was bewitched by the flashing smile and the sexuality that billowed from her. She was fifty-eight and I was twenty-six. Now a plump partridge, her soft, caressing voice (in courtesy to her British hosts she only spoke English) wove an entrancing spell around me, and I was reminded of the tempestuous affair she had had with Otto Klemperer thirty years before and which had now passed into musical folklore. All the while she sat bolt upright with ankles crossed à la Queen Mother. Indeed, it was difficult *not* to treat her as royalty.

There was supper and the wine flowed, all provided by the British hosts, for the Germans were on near starvation rations.

Then there was dancing to a very special EMI gramophone, and I danced with the lovely Clara Ebers, the principal coloratura soprano of the Hamburg State Opera.

I began to teach her the words of *Long Ago and Far Away*, for I wanted to hear that superb voice in my ear, but when I came to the line 'Thrills run up and down my spine', and I ran my fingers up and down *her* spine, she only giggled delightedly.

Then the gramophone broke down, and I noticed a colonel in the REME on his knees beside it with a screwdriver. I said, 'Do you think you can fix it, sir?'

'I ought to,' he said icily. 'I invented it.'

'Oh,' I said.

Suddenly from the grand piano in the far corner came a prodigious sound. To his own accompaniment, Rudolf Bockelmann, a famous Wotan of the '30s, began to sing

English sea shanties. This huge Wagnerian voice in a drawing-room was an experience.

Then, more dancing with Clara.

The party broke up late.

The Schumann song recital in the Musikhalle to a rapt and adoring audience was my first *live* hearing of that memorable voice, and I was in tears throughout. The voice was no longer of operatic range, but the artistry, the interpretation and the emotion were matchless.

Theo Herrmann became a particular friend. His performances of Mozart's Osmin and Strauss's Baron Ochs were renowned not only for his interpretation but his acting skills.

One afternoon in his flat the family said: 'We have a young Welshman coming round for his singing lessons; he is fantastische musicalisch.'

Enter Aircraftsman Evans, who, on being introduced to me, a captain in the Scots Guards, said, 'Good afternoon, sir.'

'Now, Geraint,' said Theo Herrmann, going to the piano, 'arpeggios.'

And then – the voice.

I still become, over fifty years later, emotional at the memory of the first hearing of that magical voice – a dark honey and brandy sound rolling effortlessly off his chest, taking in every nuance of expression and definition that Theo taught him. Geraint remained a friend for life. It was sheer magic, that first encounter.

Another memory of Hamburg after the war and friendship with the opera stars. We were listening to the formidable (and large) soprano Erna Schluter. She was talking adoringly of her young son.

'And how is Herr Schluter?' she was asked.

'There is no Herr Schluter. I wished to have a child, so I took unto me a man.'

'Das ist kein Mann.'

At a performance of *Siegfried* at Covent Garden in 1948, Set Svanholm was the eponymous hero. Duly he broke through the ring of fire to reach the sleeping Brunnhilde's side, removed the spear, then the shield, and finally the breastplate, thus revealing two mammoth mammaries. At that point the script demands he steps back and shouts startlingly, '*Das ist kein Mann!*'

But in this case Svanholm couldn't resist turning to the audience to say leeringly, '*Das ist kein Mann*'

This is the sole instance I ever experienced of the whole audience laughing at an incident in the *Ring*.

(The Brunnhilde was *not* Kirsten Flagstad.)

In the summer of 1945 our battalion was stationed near Bonn, at that time a modest town on the Rhine.

On first going there, I enquired the way, in my execrable German, to the Beethoven Haus, which turned out to be a small museum in a side street.

The only person there was the plump elderly curator. As he spoke no English, my tour of the various rooms was in silence. But as he followed me around he surely noticed my devotion to Beethoven.

We came to the room in which was the famous Broadwood piano which had been given him by the makers. I sat down on the piano stool and looked at the glass plate laid over the keyboard. I looked at the curator, he looked at me expectantly. Slowly and carefully I lifted the glass plate, and – breathlessly – played the cord of C major. I replaced the plate and looked at the curator, who was smiling and nodding his head: he knew I had had a sublime moment, playing where Beethoven had played.

That great conductor, Otto Klemperer, was rehearsing when members of the orchestra, particularly the ladies of the orchestra, noticed that all his fly-buttons were undone. Their eyes swivelled beseechingly to the leader of the orchestra, who finally got the message.

During a pause the leader whispered, 'Oh, Dr Klemperer...'

'Yess, vat iss it?'

'Your fly-buttons' (still whispering) 'they are all undone.'

'And vat hass that to do with music?' bellowed the maestro. 'We go back to bar ninety-five.'

Great conductors control orchestras by magnetism, humour and musicianship.

When John Christie built Glyndebourne opera house, he engaged Fritz Busch to conduct the very first opera to be done there, *The Marriage of Figaro.*

None of the orchestra which had been assembled had ever heard of Busch. He knew it, and he knew that he had to captivate them at once, or lose control.

At the first rehearsal, Busch took his place on the rostrum. 'Now, we begin – with the overture,' he announced. He raised his baton, the string players raised their bows. He put down his baton. 'Already too loud,' he said. Thereafter they ate out of his hand.

(Note for non-opera buffs; the overture to *Figaro* begins with pianissimo strings.)

MILITARY

The British Navy are masters of the pithy signal.

When, during the war, the liner *Queen Elizabeth* encountered the battleship *Queen Elizabeth* in mid-Atlantic, the battleship signalled 'snap'.

A destroyer captain made a hash of coming alongside the quay in Oran harbour. The flagship of the great Admiral Cunningham – C.-in-C. Mediterranean – was opposite. Help, thought the destroyer captain, I hope the old man didn't see *that*.

To his relief a flutter of flags went up on the battleship's signal halliards.

'Good,' it read, and then a pause... 'God.'

This same wonderful admiral, hearing that his second in command, Admiral Somerville, had been awarded a KCMG in addition to his KCB, signalled: 'What, twice a knight? At your age?'

The flagship of the Home Fleet was due into Portsmouth. The admiral told his flag lieutenant to go to the bridge and send a signal to his wife: 'In today, home tonight, lots of love, Rodney.'

On his way the flag lieutenant was invited to a drink by

friends in the wardroom; lonely from his work in the C.-in-C.'s quarters, he was easily persuaded to have a drink – then another – and another. So, by the time he reached the bridge to transmit the signal, he was well away.

When the admiral got home his wife gave him a puzzled look.

'What's the matter?' he asked.

She said he must be getting very odd, sending a signal like that, and handed him the text of the message: 'Home today, in tonight, lots of Rod, lovely.'

Regimental sergeant majors have had many stories told about them. RSM Archer of the Scots Guards was known as the most regimental man in the British Army. He would salute officers before talking to them on the telephone, and if he rang up a warrant officer or NCO junior to him he would shout: 'ARE YOU STANDING TO ATTENTION?'

He said to the benevolent Colonel Alan Swinton that the guardroom was becoming crowded with guardsmen and that there must be three to a cell.

'Oh, sergeant major,' said Colonel Alan, feigning innocence of the reason for this, 'why three – why not two?'

'Because sir,' barked Archer, 'two-to-a-cell-leads-to-SODOMY. Three-to-a-cell-and-they-are-bashful-SIR.'

I could fill the pages with sergeant major stories but that would be wearisome. They were, still are, a wonderful race of men. Contrary to popular belief that sergeant majors in the Brigade of Guards were harsh and inhuman, it was their very humanity and humour that got them there. The bullies and sadists were soon found out and never got promoted very far.

A single remark by an officer in The Brigade of Guards became famous in 1940 and thereafter was often repeated by my generation. The appalling drama of the British Army's evacuation from Dunkirk in May 1940 was summarised by this officer when, on his safe return to England, anxious friends asked him what it was like.

'My dears,' he said, 'the *noise* and the *people*.'

As an example of stylish insouciance it has no equal.

MONTY'S LESSON

In the late summer of 1942 Lieutenant General Bernard Montgomery of Alamein inherited command of the most professional British Army since the Peninsular War. Like Wellington's army ('by God, they frighten me') the 8th Army was far removed from Whitehall orthodoxy, and they had a spirit that came from years of shared experience living in the desert.

The Guards Brigade in this army had been in Egypt before the war started; if any formation could be accused of 'having sand in their shoes' it was them.

We were re-forming in Syria at the time of Alamein when

49

I joined the Scots Guards battalion in the brigade. We set off in pursuit up the long desert road in January 1943. The guardsmen were delighted to get back into the sand which they knew so well. We newcomers – under their tuition – learnt fast how to live in the desert.

General Montgomery had by now established himself and created the 'Monty' legend. Unlike most generals he played to the gallery. He was a professional soldier and a professional performer.

And so to Tunisia after a 2,000-mile drive along the North African Coast, where we took up anti-tank positions at Medenine for the anticipated counter-attack by Rommel's panzer divisions (the Ultra code-breakers had picked this up).

We had a fine old to-do in what Monty later described as the perfect one-day battle.

Two days after the battle Monty paid our battalion a visit to see what we had done, for we were still occupying the positions in which we had knocked out 15 German tanks.

'F' Company, with my platoon of four 6-pounder anti-tank guns, occupied the centre of the battalion defence line, and it was to the headquarters of the company in an olive grove that we had to report to meet the general.

He arrived punctually at 10am in a Honey tank, accompanied by a fleet of wireless trucks with aerials 18 feet high. The Honey tank parked decently invisible in the olive grove, but the wireless trucks were strung out along the track on a forward slope. A tempting target for the German 88-mm guns. Sure enough, we heard the whine of the first shell arriving. It exploded impeccably on range but 50 yards off the main target.

'Hullo,' piped Monty, jumping on to his tank and pulling out his field glasses (what *did* he expect to see?). 'Are they shooting at me?'

Yes, was our unspoken thought, and us too, and we *live* here.

'Don't you think, sir,' said Major General Bobby Erskine, 'that we had better go down there [pointing] out of sight?'

'Driver, DRIVE ON,' he commanded as two more shells arrived.

So we trooped off to the dead ground where my guns were sited.

I had been told that I was to take the general round my gun positions. Monty made a few nice remarks to each gun crew as they stood properly dressed in peaked caps in the gun pits while each gun commander gave a concise account of his actions. So far so good – a normal army commander's inspection – but we had yet to visit my forward gun, commanded by Sergeant 'Tasher' McDonald. I didn't know what to expect, but it was bound to be out of the ordinary.

As we approached the gun my heart sank. Sergeant McDonald was benevolently watching his gun crew, who were stripped to the waist and hacking away purposefully with pick and shovel, making improvements to a gun pit that needed no improving. There he stood, brasses gleaming, his great red moustache like a fire in the sunlight. Even his *back* view expressed the light of mischief I knew to be in his eye.

Monty, with the accompanying entourage of brass hats, colonels and me, arrived. Sergeant McDonald pretended to notice us for the first time and thundered to attention, brought up the gun crew with a barked order and peeled off a prodigious salute.

'Well, sergeant,' asked Monty, 'and what happened here in the battle?'

'It was like this, sir...' began McDonald. There followed a lurid description, in which there was some fact buried among the fancy. Suddenly he broke off with a dramatic gesture –

'Ah, it's nae good ye just standing there, sir. Come doon here if ye will, and I can explain better if ye'll just get behind the sights.'

Monty meekly complied, crouching down in the gun-layer's

51

position. McDonald placed his great hands paternally on Monty's shoulders.

'Now, sir, if ye'll just traverse a wee bit tae the right,' (*pushing* him round). 'There noo, steady on that; ye see yon tankie on the ridge? He came up ower the horizon for a' the worrld like a submariney cooming oot the watter' (the accent was getting broader).

Everyone among the little knot of senior officers was speechless as McDonald continued to instruct Monty in the niceties of knocking out every tank in sight. General Erskine turned to me and whispered, 'This is terrific. I came round to see this man of yours yesterday and he told me a completely different story – but this one is even better!'

Poor Monty was getting restless. Sergeant McDonald's mouth was twitching mirthfully as he warmed to the task of spinning out his fantasy. His gun crew stood immobile, respectful, registering nothing.

But Monty had had enough. Somehow evading the hands that held him he got to his feet, dusting sand off his knees.

'Yes, yes,' he said, routed and retreating, 'quite, quite, sergeant. I understand, thank you, thank you.'

Sergeant McDonald realised he was losing his pupil, so once more the crew were snapped to attention, once more the prodigious salute. And then came the punchline.

'THANK YOU VERY MUCH FAE THE VISIT, SIR, AND *DO* COME AGAIN'

Monty quickly recovered his composure after his encounter with Sergeant McDonald. He asked for as many men as were in the vicinity to gather round. Some 40 or 50 men and officers were on hand. Monty then gave us a talk, telling us that he didn't believe in failure, and that he was going to drive the Germans out of Africa.

Those of us officers in this group became hot and embarrassed: it was like the headmaster of a prep. school giving a pep talk to the rugger XV.

When he had left (in his Honey tank) one of our tough old desert sergeants came up to me, his eyes shining. 'Wasn't the general *marvellous*, sir.'

The penny dropped. The talk was aimed at the guardsmen, not the officers. Monty, the canny PR man, knew where and how to raise spirits.

MISCELLANY

In 1944 the German forces occupying Hungary were unpopular with their easygoing Hungarian allies. The first-class compartment in a train had four passengers, one in each corner. They were – an elderly Hungarian countess, a beautiful girl, a German officer and a Hungarian officer. There were no lights in the compartment so when the train entered a tunnel it was in darkness.

Came the sound of a succulent kiss, followed by a violent slap. When the train came out of the tunnel everyone was still in their place, but the German had a red cheek and a black eye.

The old lady thought, what a good girl to resist the advances of that aggressive-looking German.

The girl thought, pity, I rather fancied that attractive German and the silly man kisses the old lady.

The German thought, that swinish Hungarian has a go at the girl and I get hit for it.

The Hungarian thought, I'm a smart fellow, I kiss the back of my hand, hit a German and get away with it.

> How does the bride spell groom?
> Gee – ahhr – oh – OH! mmm

A very grand elderly peer was approached by a charity worker bent on collecting for a sale.

'What do you do with your old clothes?' asked the earnest fellow.

'I take them off at night, and then I put them on again in the morning.'

If you (as a man) find yourself trapped among a gaggle of women all yacking away, wait for a pause and say: 'Women enjoy knitting because it gives them something to think about when they are talking.' Then get ready to duck.

I had 12 bottles of whisky in my cellar and was told by my wife to empty the contents of each bottle down the sink, or else. So I said I would, and proceeded with the unpleasant task.

I withdrew the cork from the first bottle, poured the contents down the sink with the exception of one glass, which I drank.

I pulled the cork from the second bottle and did likewise with the exception of one glass, which I drank.

I extracted the cork from the third bottle and poured the whisky down the sink, which I drank.

I extracted the cork from the fourth bottle down the sink and poured the bottle down the glass, which I drank.

I poured the bottle down the cork of the next and drank one sink of it and poured the rest down the glass.

I pulled the sink out of the next glass and poured the cork down the bottle.

Then I corked the sink with the glass, bottled the drink and drank the pour.

When I had everything emptied I steadied the house with one hand and counted the glasses, corks, bottles and sinks with the other, there were 29.

As the house came by I counted the glasses, corks and all the bottles in the house, which I drank.

I am not under the affluence of incohol but some think people I am.

I am not half so think as I might drink. I fool so feelish I don't know who is me and the drinker I stand here the longer I get.

(Anon)

A man had an obsession for catapults: he had never put away the childish delight in twanging conkers into the rumps of unsuspecting elderly ladies.

So he had to go to an asylum, he had become a nuisance. Time went by, psychiatrists worked on him. And then the day came when they considered him normal and ready to go back to the outside world.

The man took the news calmly.

'Now,' asked the doctors, 'what will you do when we release you?'

'I will try and find a nice good-looking girl,' he said.

The doctors were thrilled.

'Then,' he continued, 'I would take her into a glade in a wood, and ask her to lie down.'

'Yes, yes,' nodded the doctors expectantly.

'I would lift up her skirts, take off her knickers...'

'Yes, yes, go on...'

'...and take out the elastic and make a catapult.'

An eminent London art dealer to a Jewish ditto:

'After all, an Arab is only a Jew on a horse.'

A member of White's Club, known for his prodigious drinking habits, was seen coming down the beautiful eighteenth-century staircase on his hands and knees.

'Goodness, what *are* you doing?' they asked.

'I'm God, moving in a mysterious way.'

…As the hurricane said to the palm tree, 'Hold on to your nuts, this is no ordinary blow-through.'

The hospitals' rugby cup final was a great event; young doctors working off energy.

The final between Bart's and St Mary's one year was made for one doctor: he was the wing three-quarter who took a pass, knocked it on but re-caught it, the referee didn't see it, and he scored the winning try for Bart's.

This preyed on his conscience all his life so that when he died the first thing he did at the pearly gates was to confess, 'Oh, St Peter, I cheated in that important rugger match – my try was not disallowed and it should have been.'

'My boy, from up here we look down and see everything: of course you took the ball cleanly and your winning try was legitimate. Oh, and by the way, St Peter is on holiday and I'm his stand-in, St Bartholomew.'

In the days of the Indian Empire people and troops went to the hill stations in summer to escape the heat.

The colonel of a regiment at a hill station was called to Delhi for a conference. He asked one of his more personable subalterns to be kind to his wife.

She – an attractive woman – invited the young man to dinner, just the two of them. After a good dinner by candlelight they sat on the sofa drinking liqueurs. She said to him, 'Can you spell opportunity?'

He, recounting the story in later life, said, 'And like a bloody fool, I spelt it.'

In the early 1950s the French had got round to corduroy trousers, a case of clothes fashion crossing the Channel in reverse order. A smart shop in the Rue de Rivoli in Paris displayed corduroy trousers in the window with the sales slogan: '*Il y a très snob, presque cad.*'

In January 1958 my wife and I stayed in Vienna as guests of American friends: he was a Bostonian of the 1630 vintage. She had very grand Hungarian ancestry but was a fully assimilated American. Through her we made friends with poverty stricken Hungarians and Austrians with names like Berchtold and Radetski. We ourselves were still Mr and Mrs Gordon.

One day ten of us went to Eisenstadt in a convoy of ancient cars. When we had done the sights we went to a gasthaus for lunch. Our self-appointed leader was Count Louis Berchtold, an imposing man of 60 with an astrakhan coat and hat. ('Das ist der Furst!' cried the street urchins.)

The staff at the gasthaus were thrown into a flurry by all these grand folk arriving. Tables were put together and Louis Berchtold said: 'And now we must arrange the seating by protocol.' He spoke lightly, even humorously, for the benefit of the American and British couples, but nevertheless he meant it, as did all the other remains of the Austro-Hungarian Empire.

After we had been seated – by protocol – Louis turned to the American lady, alarmed that he might not have got the pecking order exactly right. 'Tell me,' he asked, 'who was Mrs Gordon's grandmother on her mother's side?'

When I was a new boy at Harrow, I, like most other boys at the school, would sometimes sit on a high stool at the food bar of 'the Hill' (the school tuck shop). This bar was presided over by a chirpy cockney sparrow called Charlie. On a particular day I was trying to look invisible because beside me was a *very* grand senior boy – the Maharajah of Cooch Behar. He was spraying masses of pepper over his plate of egg and chips. Charlie observed him intently and said:

'Hey, watch it, Cooch – any more of that and you'll set yer arse on fire when you fart.'